MAYE'S MARCH FOR WOMEN'S VOTES

By
Amy Houts

Houts & Home Publications LLC
Maryville, Missouri

*Dedicated to Mary Hertz Scarbrough,
whose interest in suffrage sparked my own,
and to the many brave women and men
who fought for women's voting rights.*

Cover Design: Meggan Houts
Interior design: Meggan Houts

© 2021 Amy Houts
All rights reserved. No part of this publication may be reproduced, stored in retrieval systems, or transmitted in any form or by any means, electronic, photocopying, mechanical, recording, or otherwise, without prior
written permission of Amy Houts or
Houts & Home Publications LLC.

Printed in the United States of America
ISBN: 978-0-9855084-7-0

Library of Congress Control Number: 2020900485

For inquiries contact:
Amy Houts, President
Houts & Home Publications LLC
26162 Ridge Drive
Maryville, Missouri 64468
Cell phone: 660.582.1426
Email: houtsandhome@gmail.com
Website: www.houtsandhome.com

Table of Contents

Chapter 1: A New Possibility — 7
Chapter 2: The "Antis" — 13
Chapter 3: A Thousand Miles — 18
Chapter 4: An Unruly Crowd — 28
Chapter 5: A Ladies Band Leads — 30
A Brief History — 39
Index — 49
Image Credits — 51
Bibliography — 55

Acknowledgements

There are so many people to thank for creating this book—from the summer of 2013 when I started until I decided to publish it myself in 2020. My dear friend Mary Hertz Scarbrough's passion for the suffrage movement was contagious. Thank you, Mary, for starting me on this journey and for believing in me. I couldn't have done it without your encouragement, support, and friendship. Big thanks to Melissa Middleswart, who spent countless hours at the Nodaway County Historical Museum helping me to research Vera Maye Shipps and the Missouri Ladies Military Band. Thank you to NCHM staff (Margaret Kelley and Cathy Palmer) and volunteers at the museum, too. Thank you to those who read my manuscript even though they didn't know me especially, Thomas Carneal, Professor Emeritus of History, Northwest Missouri State University, Maryville, Missouri, Nodaway County Historian. And to those who know me best, my mother, Betty Farber (who read many manuscript several times through different revisions!) and my sister, Nancy Browning, who not only read, but edited the manuscript meticulously more than once. Thank you! Literary agent, Janet Reid of New Leaf Media, you were so encouraging about my taking time to make revisions and develop Maye's character (even though I wasn't your client—thank you, Janet!). I'm so grateful to you, Karen Pavlicin-Fragnito, publisher at Elva Resa, for the chance to get your feedback and nearly(!) secure a contract. Your belief in this story gave me confidence. Thanks to Naomi Krueger, editor at Beaming Books, for helping me to develop a rhyming picture book version and seriously considering publishing it. And for your suggestion, Cheryl B. Klein, (at the time) Arthur A. Levine editor, that I self-publish this book as a regional title. That's what I ultimately decided to do. I couldn't forget my husband, Steve, and his support, kindness, and patience over the years of manuscript submissions, rejections, and heartache. Special thanks to Mary Seat for taking photos of her trombone, to Coby Lamb, for the use of his postcards of the Ladies Band featuring "Mary Villemo," the Wabash depot, and downtown Maryville, and to Phil Cobb, owner and publisher of the Maryville Forum newspaper for giving me permission to print the front page from March 1, 1913. I'm sure there are others that I've forgotten to mention here, but I'm grateful for you all. It's been quite a journey!

Vera Maye Shipps

A New Possibility
Chapter 1

Like many women in the early 1900s, Vera Maye Shipps wanted to vote. Men voted. Why not women? Her father voted. Her brothers voted. *It isn't fair!* thought Maye, as she was called. *Women are required to live according to laws made by men. Women should be able to vote on the laws that affect us.*

Maryville, Missouri, early 1900s

In the small Midwestern town of Maryville, Missouri, near her family's farm, there wasn't much Maye could do to advance women's voting rights, called "suffrage." Granted, she could attend a meeting, listen to a lecture, and stay informed by reading the newspaper. But she wanted to do something more, something important, something big or small to make a difference in the fight for suffrage.

So, when Maye was asked to march in a parade to support suffrage, she was ready to go. This was no small request. The parade would take place in Washington, DC, halfway across the country and a world away from Northwest Missouri. Maye would participate in the parade as a member of the Missouri Ladies Military Band—if the band was able to make the trip. The parade was scheduled for March 3, 1913, the day before the presidential inauguration of Woodrow Wilson.

The band's director, Miss Alma Nash, had read an article in *The Kansas City Times* stating that the National American Woman Suffrage Association was seeking bands to march in support of women's voting rights.

"I will send a telegram this week to the person in charge of the parade to see if they will accept our band," said Miss Nash at a January band practice. Smiling broadly, Miss Nash looked as excited about the prospect as the band members.

For over two years—since Maye was 17—she and her sister Florence had traveled by sleigh in winter or hack (wagon) in summer from their farm to the music school in Maryville. Officially called The School of Banjo, Mandolin, and Guitar, 30 young women met for weekly practice as members of the Missouri Ladies Military Band. Maye and Florence often fell asleep in the sleigh after practice, but the horse knew the way home.

Miss Alma Nash's title was Directress

Maye's older brothers, Otis and Ray, had taught her to play the slide trombone. She loved the big, brassy sound. She practiced often, getting lost in the melodies. It helped her escape from everyday concerns, and hers were pretty typical for a farm girl. The youngest of nine children, Maye helped Mama in the house and Papa with outside chores. She dreamed of a home of her own someday, but her dreams didn't end there.

In 1910, when Maye read an advertisement in the newspaper seeking musicians for the Missouri Ladies Military Band, Maye knew she had the necessary training. Becoming a charter member of the band and performing with her friends was an experience like no other. It elevated her life and gave her joy. Miss Nash had called her playing "promising" and had told Maye if she kept it up, she would be accomplished enough to play with a professional band.

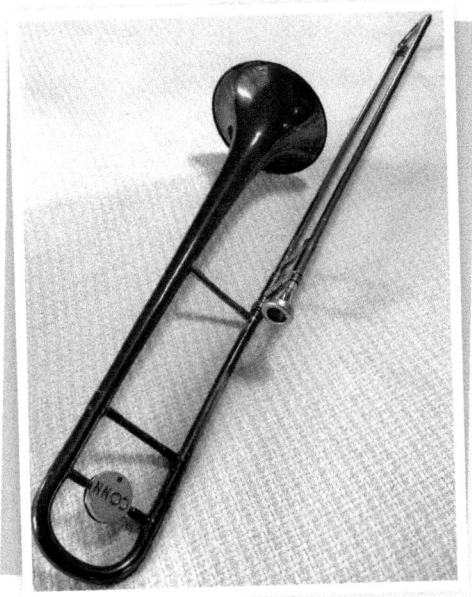

Maye called this musical instrument a "slide trombone," which was later shortened to trombone.

Wabash Railroad Depot, Maryville, Missouri

Maye had seldom traveled far. That was one reason she had joined the band. Traveling by train—nearly every small town had their own railroad depot—the Ladies Band had performed in Missouri, Iowa, and Nebraska, in towns that Maye would have never otherwise visited. Each performance brought new surprises, which she recorded in her diary. After a trip to Higginsville, Missouri, "*a young man fell desperately in love with me, proposing marriage most heartily.*" Of course, she had to disappoint him.

The girls readied their musical instrument sections: percussion, brass, and woodwind. Maye chatted excitedly with her best friend, Ora Quinn, about this new possibility. If they were able to attend, the railroad trip to the suffrage parade would be the farthest she had ever traveled! *I can't wait to tell Mama and Papa*, thought Maye as she blew into her slide trombone to warm it. Ora assembled the pieces of her B-flat clarinet. Orlena Helpley started the rhythm by banging her mallet on the bass drum. Soon, music filled the room as the band practiced an upbeat, patriotic march, John Philip Sousa's "The Stars and Stripes Forever."

Thinking over the last two years, Maye wrote in her diary:

[Undated]
[Joining the band] might be called the turning point in my life events. The traveling, new towns and places, getting acquainted with new people [have been] a constant source of education and enjoyment.

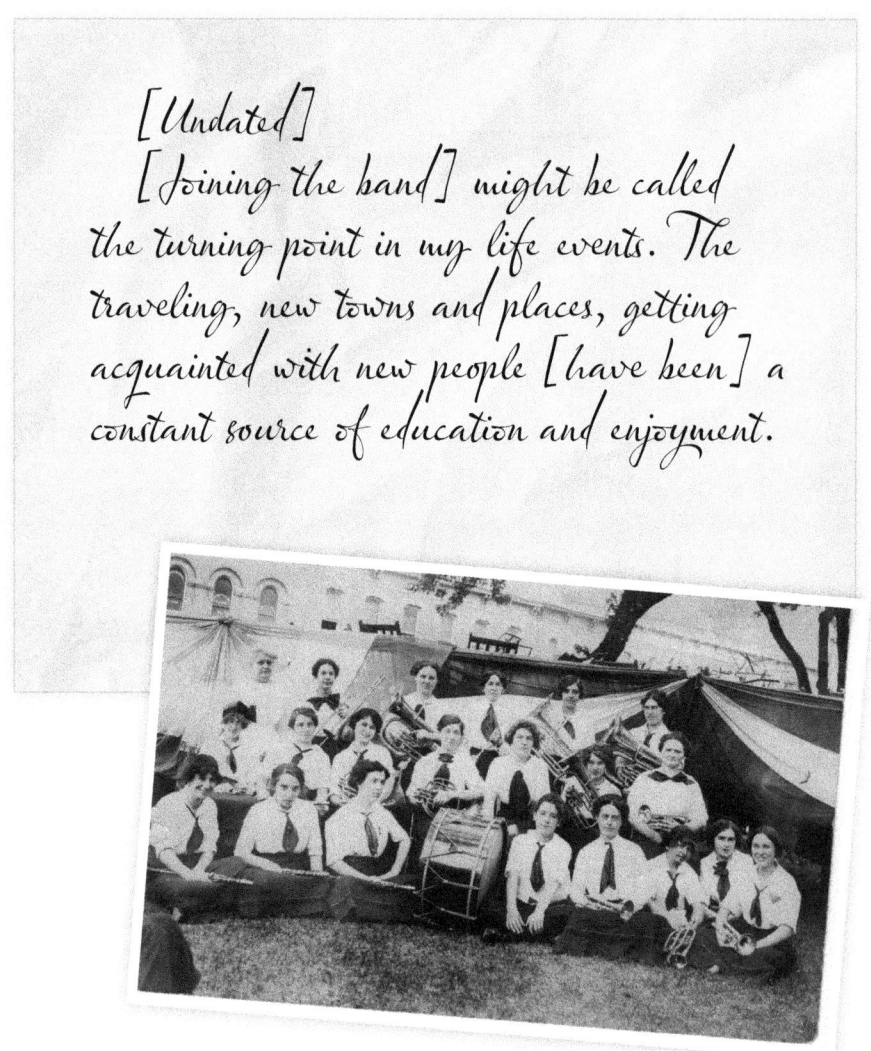

The Missouri Ladies Military Band, circa 1910

The "Antis"
Chapter 2

At the next practice, Miss Nash told the band members the good news. "I sent a telegram to the person in charge of the states' delegations and heard from Elizabeth Kent, chairman of the committee on bands." Miss Nash read the telegram. " 'We should be delighted to have a ladies band in our parade'."

This Western Union telegram is dated 1913.

Miss Nash paused until the young ladies had gained their composure.

She continued, " 'Your band is the only one which professes an interest in suffrage and is willing to come for expenses to Washington'."

"Come for expenses" meant part of their trip was paid for. Band members would need to raise money for the majority of the cost of their railroad tickets and other expenses. The band would not be paid like the other bands, which were professional. The band members had a lot of work to do and just over a month to prepare. In addition, they would need to learn to march.

Until that day, the Missouri Ladies Military Band had been a concert band, sitting to play their music. Standing and walking while playing a musical instrument would take practice, and they would need a larger space than the music school could offer.

This concert band sat to play music.

Maye and the other band members braved the snow that February for extra time to rehearse. Because of the winter weather, they were unable to practice outside. So Miss Nash petitioned local businesses for a space to march. She was given permission to use Woodman Hall, which was not far from the music school. The large hall in downtown Maryville was located on the third floor of an attorney's office building. There was more than enough room for the band to practice their steps. Maye loved the work. Marching and playing reminded her of dancing. The lively pieces the band played made her want to get up on her feet and move!

Would they be ready in time? Maye wondered, abundantly aware of a more pressing concern. *Would they raise sufficient funds for the trip?*

Edna F. Gellhorn, Missouri Equal Suffrage League

Edna F. Gellhorn of St. Louis sent the band a letter stating that the Missouri Equal Suffrage League would set aside $150 for expenses. The band combined their treasury of $70 with their donations: $550 from suffrage organizations and $300 from families in the community. However, the total was not enough to purchase 25 railroad tickets and cover other expenses. Miss Nash said she would canvass local businesses but couldn't promise success.

As news spread of the upcoming event, many people in the community were proud of the efforts "our girls" were making. They believed it was time for women to vote and felt that the nation would benefit by women having a say in government. But others believed it would ruin the family. They were called the "antis" because they were anti-suffrage. They thought women were innocent and pure and belonged at home taking care of their families, not out in public voting. Editorials for and against women's suffrage were published in the Maryville *Daily Democrat-Forum*.

The Ladies Band made the front page of Maryville's newspaper, the Daily Democrat Forum, March 1, 1913 with the headline "WEPT AT PARTING."

Newspaper articles kept the community apprised of the band's progress. Miss Nash was questioned by a reporter who obviously disapproved. The reporter stated that at colleges and universities, male students performed in marching bands. Men marched in parades. Women did not. Miss Nash was far from discouraged, but she carefully worded her reply.

"The suffrage officers seemed to think the novelty of a lady's band is sufficient to overcome any opposition. In fact, they have asked us to march at the head of the procession," Miss Nash said.

She didn't tell the reporter they were still short on funds. After exhausting all other possibilities, Miss Nash visited the bank for a loan, which her father had to co-sign. She estimated they would need another $170. It was a lot of money, but she couldn't let the band members down. She vowed to book band concerts at picnics, fairs, and festivals all summer to pay back the loan.

A Thousand Miles
Chapter 3

On a cold morning, Saturday, March 1, Mama and Papa drove Maye and Florence in the sleigh to the Wabash Train Station in Maryville. There they joined half the town, a crowd of well-wishers saying their goodbyes. Alma Nash's little sister, 14-year old Elizabeth, was teary-eyed showing a friend the pages in her notebook containing the names and addresses to whom she promised to send postcards. Maye was surprised by Elizabeth's sadness because her mother and sister would accompany her. Unlike Elizabeth, the parents of other band members tried to hide their last-minute reluctance, instead giving cautious advice regarding safety.

The Missouri Ladies Military Band before they boarded the train for Washington, DC.

A photographer asked the young ladies to gather together. He took a photo of the band members dressed in their wool coats and hats, some trimmed in beaver fur. Each band member carried her musical instrument and a small suitcase because their trunks of clothing had been shipped ahead of time for the seven-day trip. Maye's suitcase held her diary. The train pulled out of the station at 10:52 a.m.

When the train started moving, Maye caught her breath. They were finally on their way! She couldn't believe it. They were going to travel for two days, over 1,000 miles, from the northwest corner of Missouri to the heart of Washington, DC, to march in a grand parade. They would eat in the dining car and sleep on the train.

"This is such a lark!" said Ora, as Maye nodded in agreement.

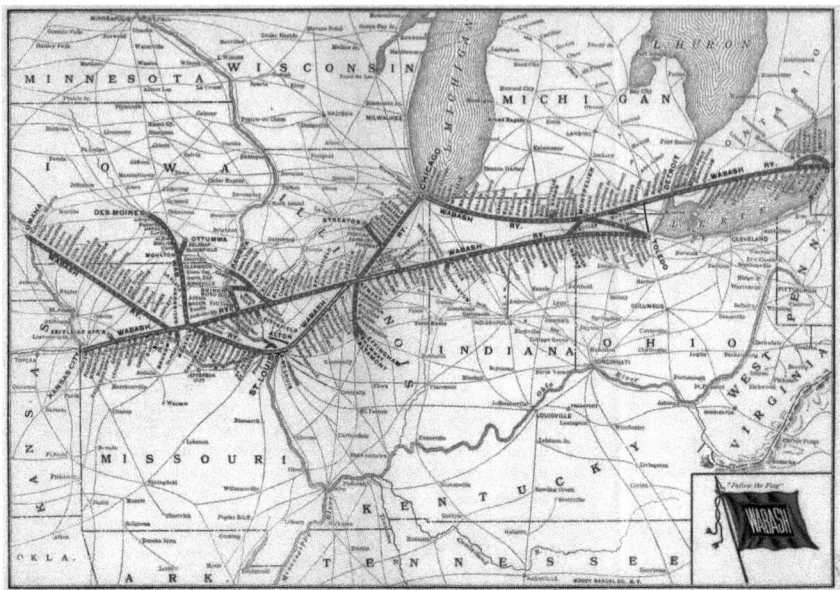

The first train the band rode transported them from Maryville to St. Louis.

Maye sat by the window, the railroad car gently rocking to and fro. In all her 19 years, she had never traveled this far from home. *There is a whole world I have not yet experienced*, Maye thought, feeling very lucky she was on this trip. But she couldn't daydream for long.

"Young ladies," said Miss Nash. Even though her rigorous training prepared them well, Miss Nash required the band to practice once again. After running through their repertoire, Miss Nash was satisfied and allowed the women free time. With the upbeat songs playing silently in her mind, Maye relaxed, looking out the window at the tree-lined fields and split rail fences. As she wrote a postcard to Mama and Papa, Mr. Steeg, the passenger agent, brought coffee to the ladies in her group. The farmland, with its towering silos, gave way to country towns.

The women in the band sold this postcard of themselves on the train as a fundraiser. It includes a song dedicated to their hometown, Maryville, featuring a person named Mary Villemo. "MO" is the post office's abbreviation for Missouri.

She glanced at Elizabeth Nash, who was busy writing postcards, her tears gone. Maye searched her heart and found no regret, homesickness, or fear—only anticipation and excitement. Yet, the reason for the trip was always in the back of her mind. Maye wondered, *Would the parade make a difference in the struggle for voting rights?*

A man in a uniform punched Maye's railway ticket.

That evening, Maye recorded the highlights in her diary:

> March 1st, 1913.
> Five-minute stop at Moberly, Missouri. Ora and I ran into the depot. After posting my card for Mama and Papa, we flirted with the clerk through the window. Supper at 7 o'clock. Ora won honors for eating the most olives and I for causing the most pickles to disappear.

Country towns gave way to city lights. Maye gazed at lamps shining in the darkness. At 11 o'clock, they arrived in St. Louis to change trains. A group of suffragists presented the band with a five-pound box of fine candies that included a note from Mrs. George Gellhorn of the Missouri Equal Suffrage League.

"My Dear Miss Nash: We regret so much that your late arrival will prevent our meeting you and the members of your party. We had hoped you could come early for a little demonstration at the station. Since this is impossible, will you accept this box of sweets with our heartfelt good wishes for a successful trip? Sincerely, Edna F. Gellhorn."

"I suppose they thought you were not sweet enough," said a reporter from the *St. Louis Star*, making the girls giggle.

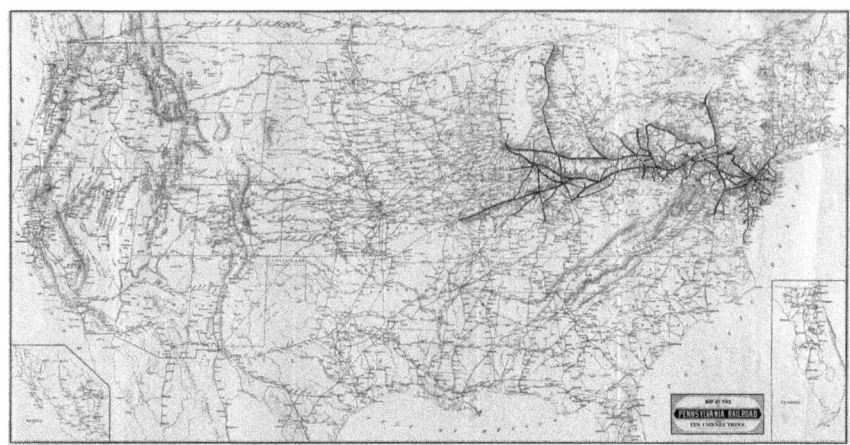

This Pennsylvania railroad map shows the route from St. Louis to Washington, DC.

In St. Louis, Maye admired Union Station as an agent of the Pennsylvania Railroad escorted her group to a Pullman railway car. The berths were made up, ready for them to sleep. But Maye didn't sleep well because of the *"constant thunderous bumps and creaking of breaks* [sic]."

By 8 A.M., when the train stopped in Indianapolis, Indiana, Maye and Ora were dressed and ready. She, along with several of the young ladies, left the train to buy cards. Maye became distracted and lost track of time. Luckily, she heard the porter as he yelled, "Last call! All aboard!" Maye and Ora picked up their skirts and ran as fast as they could, stepping onboard just before the train started moving.

Maye recorded the sights in her diary:

> a great number of oil derricks. Passing through Dayton, Ohio, a large manufacturing city with smoke billowing out of factory towers and the foreboding penitentiary wall at Columbus.

Maye saw the Steubenville, Ohio ironworks from the train window—one of many interesting sights on her trip.

That afternoon, Miss Nash invited passengers from other cars to attend a band concert. They took up a generous collection that totaled $4.00, enough to buy cake for everyone in the band with money left over. But Miss Nash didn't splurge on dessert; she used it to help defray practical expenses.

The train rumbled through six long, dark tunnels. Then they arrived at Steubenville, a large town with extensive ironworks. Dusk turned to darkness shortly after.

In the evening, Maye wrote in her diary:

> March 2nd, 1913.
> Arrived in Pittsburg 7 P.M. A grand station there. A passenger agent escorted us through the brilliantly lighted streets of the town to the DeQueen Hotel where we enjoyed a fine supper.

The train left Pittsburg at 11:15 P.M. This time Maye slept well, but others were not so fortunate.

"I was sick last night," said Florence. "All the winding through the mountains!"

Eating in a dining car was an experience.

The morning of March 3, Maye and Ora awoke early. Passengers crowded the dining car so Maye and her friend were unable to order breakfast. As the train entered Washington, DC, Maye glimpsed the dome of the Capitol and the pencil-shaped Washington Monument in the distance. They had finally arrived!

An Unruly Crowd
Chapter 4

    A man from their home town, Mr. Van Cleve, met them at the beautiful new Union Station. Van Cleve, a clerk for a Missouri congressman, lived in Washington, DC, part of the year. Maye and the others joined those on the already crowded sidewalks. Thousands of out-of-towners were visiting that week for the presidential inauguration of Woodrow Wilson. Streetcars, automobiles, and horses and buggies shuttled visitors on paved roads. Maye thrilled to the sights and sounds; the city had a rhythm and music all its own. It was such a contrast to the quiet courthouse square of Maryville's tiny downtown, with its brick, dusty gravel, or mud roads.

The hotels were full, so makeshift boarding houses were provided for the visitors. Mr. Van Cleve escorted the young women to a converted beauty parlor furnished with cots at a cost of $1.75 per day. Luckily, it was within easy walking distance of the Capitol. There was no time to rest after their long trip. The parade was scheduled to begin at 3 o'clock.

Maye later recorded the preparations in her diary.

> March 3rd, 1913.
> After our dinner at 12 noon, we donned our uniforms with great care, gave our instruments a final polish, and made certain we were in prime condition, then proceeded to the Peace Monument where we formed in line for the greatest parade of that nature ever given up until that time.

The young women walked in groups or pairs. Maye could hardly breathe, she was so excited. The day she had worked for had arrived. Today she would march for women's suffrage.

The members of the Ladies Band walked from the boarding house to the Peace Monument on the Capitol grounds, instruments in hand. Leading the parade was Miss Inez Milholland, seated on a white horse. A number of the National American Woman Suffrage Association officers rode chestnut horses, and others were on foot. The women wore classical robes and gowns in the Greek and Roman style. The Missouri Ladies Military Band was next in line.

Inez Milholland led the parade.

Maye's navy blue serge uniform, a skirt and long-sleeved jacket with black trim, kept off the chill. All the ladies in their band dressed in the same blue serge trimmed with a thick, black braid. While she was waiting for the parade to begin, Maye chatted with Ora about all they had seen: the costumes, banners, and floats. The parade looked massive, trailing on as far as they could see.

As they waited in formation, a crowd gathered on the sidewalk. The crowds, mostly of men, watched the ladies intently as the men checked their pocket watches. Everyone waited. The parade did not start at 3 o'clock as planned. Men pressed against the thick, wire cable separating the spectators from the marchers. Maye tried not to stare at anyone in particular. Something about the crowd made her wary. Her intuition told her something was happening, but she wasn't quite sure what. *Probably just the excitement*, she thought. Looking at the crowd, she saw sneers and looks of contempt. A crowd this size could get out of hand. A policeman standing nearby gave her confidence. The police would keep order.

The National American Woman Suffrage Association officers led the parade.

The Missouri Ladies Military Band marching in the parade in Washington, DC on March 3, 1913

When the suffrage officers started moving forward, Miss Nash signaled the downbeat. Sunlight sparkled on the polished brass of Maye's slide trombone. The Missouri Ladies Military Band marched as they played patriotic music. The crowd's cheering and clapping thrilled Maye as she marched in step. The music took her to a special place away from her concerns. Maybe she was wrong—maybe the men were there for support. *It would have been fun to be a spectator to observe the great event*, she thought.

After the band had marched a short distance, a steel cable separating the spectators from the marchers snapped. The crowd closed in. Maye froze. A policeman stood nearby, his arms folded. *Why won't he help?* Maye wondered. Men blockaded the street ahead. The happy cheering turned to angry insults.

A Ladies Band Leads
Chapter 5

One of the suffrage officers came rushing back. "Go on ahead!" she yelled to Miss Nash and the band, waving them on with a sweep of her arm. "You will need to open the way."

Miss Nash did not hesitate as she led the band, directing Maye and the other young women to keep marching. Maye stood tall as they approached the blockade. Maye played her slide trombone with great intent. The band played on, and the music worked its magic, soothing the crowd. The band played its whole repertoire, entrancing bystanders who wished the parade would go no further.

Spectators crowded the streets.

Finally, the men dispersed. No one prevented the band from continuing. Maye sighed with relief. She found out later from newspaper reports that men hired by anti-suffragists to disrupt the event had tripped, grabbed, and pushed marchers. More than 100 of the injured were taken to the hospital. When the Fort Myer Cavalry arrived, the marchers continued to complete the parade route, with an estimated 250,000 spectators. The Missouri Ladies Military Band didn't see the fighting because it was behind them.

Maye marched down Pennsylvania Avenue, where she hoped to see the White House. Progress was slow because of the pressing crowds, but the band didn't stop until they reached the Treasury Building. They had walked for miles. Maye was exhausted but happy. And the days' events were far from over.

Dramas, speeches, and music fueled the celebration.

One of the speakers, author and activist Helen Keller—who was deaf and blind—was so shaken by the disruption during the parade that she was unable to give her speech. The Missouri Ladies Military Band played national anthems from a number of the represented countries for the suffrage meeting in the Continental Congress building. The band members met Dr. Anna Howard Shaw, president of the National American Woman Suffrage Association. Maye was honored to meet Dr. Shaw, a leader of the cause. *With so many good people working for suffrage, how could it fail?* Maye wondered.

Maye wrote in her diary of the evening's events:

> March 3rd, 1913.
> [With] supper over, we went out again [and] saw the great preparation for the inaugural parade of the morrow. Great flights of seats and boxes, vine- and flower-trimmed, all along Pennsylvania Ave.

There was no evidence of the suffrage parade, as if it had never happened. But Maye would never forget it. It gave her life new meaning.

Maye's role changed from performer to spectator and tourist as the band members watched the inaugural parade

President Woodrow Wilson

and then visited the White House and George Washington's home, Mount Vernon. With a wistful reluctance to leave, Maye said goodbye to the picturesque city.

Maye wrote in her diary:

> March 6th, 1913. Back on the train to Missouri beginning Thursday morning. Much beautiful scenery all day in the Susquehanna Valley.
>
> March 7th, 1913. Spent most of Friday shopping in St. Louis. Bought a new green spring hat.
>
> March 8th, 1913. Arrived in Maryville at 6 A.M., a tired but thoroughly satisfied bunch with much to tell.

When they disembarked from the train in Maryville, reporters gathered around.

"We did not have time to stop and think about the really important thing we did when our band led the parade down Pennsylvania Avenue," said Miss Nash, relating the story of the blockade. "That it would be necessary for the band to open the way proved true."

Maye smiled. She had longed to do something to make a difference in the fight for suffrage, and she had succeeded. The memory of her experience would last a lifetime.

A Brief History

This book is based on a real event, real people, and a real band. The Missouri Ladies Military Band traveled 1,000 miles by train to Washington, DC, to march in the "Woman Suffrage Procession" in 1913. One of the band members, Vera Maye Shipps, kept a diary. Her diary was the basis for this book.

In big cities and small towns in every state and in territories that would become part of the US, people fought for women to have "suffrage," the right to vote. Maryville, Missouri, was one of those small towns. Women important to the suffrage movement toured the country, traveling by automobile, railroad, steamship, buggy, horseback, or on foot, to give lectures. In fact, over 35 years before the parade, in 1876, suffrage leader Susan B. Anthony had spoken in Maryville. She had said "that men, no matter how ignorant, could vote. But women, no matter how educated, could not have anything to do with [the] making of any law."

Susan B. Anthony fought for suffrage most of her life.

In 1913, Maryville, 100 miles north of Kansas City and 50 miles north of the booming town of St. Joseph, had a population of 4,000. This progressive town had started a teachers college in 1905. Clubs formed in Northwest Missouri, first to promote temperance to limit alcohol, and later, to include work for women's rights. Their members raised money for these causes and invited women important to the suffrage movement to lecture in Maryville. Elizabeth Cady Stanton spoke in 1879, and Dr. Anna Howard Shaw spoke in 1901 and 1902. Maye was eight years old when Dr. Shaw gave her speech on women's suffrage in Maryville, but there is no record as to whether Maye or anyone in her family attended the speech. (Author's note: I'd like to imagine that she did.) Growing up during the push for women's voting rights and participating in the 1913 parade gave Maye's life a unique focus.

The front cover of the suffrage parade program

This important parade renewed interest and energy in fighting for women's voting rights. Interest had dwindled because the suffrage movement stretched over 60 years, since the first National Women's Rights Convention in 1848. By 1913, many of the early leaders, such as Susan B. Anthony and Elizabeth Cady Stanton, were dead.

Alice Paul   *Lucy Burns*

After fighting for suffrage in Britain, young, educated leaders Alice Paul and Lucy Burns returned to the US to work for the National American Woman Suffrage Association (NAWSA). They started planning and advertising the parade, their first event for the NAWSA, in December of 1912. They had only a few months to organize a large-scale parade of 5,000 marchers, nine bands, four sets of horseback riders, and 24 floats—the biggest ever in Washington, DC. Miss Paul planned the date of the event to be the day before Woodrow Wilson's inauguration to ensure that thousands of people would be visiting the city.

A 20-page program was printed by the NAWSA for the extravagant parade, which cost more than $14,000 at a time when the average yearly income was $621. Reporters covered notable marchers, such as "General" Rosalie Jones and her "Suffrage Pilgrims," who had traveled 20 days from New York to participate. One pilgrim drove a bright yellow, horse-drawn wagon full of information on women's suffrage, which she handed out on the way.

However, most of the publicity about the parade was printed after it took place. With hundreds of thousands of spectators, rowdy behavior, and little police protection, dozens of marchers were hospitalized. Ambulances worked for six hours to deliver the injured. Congressional hearings lasted for weeks, with testimony centering on the lack of police protection. The chief of the Washington, DC, police, Major Richard Sylvester, was thoroughly questioned at the hearings. Afterwards, he was fired.

Because of the way women were treated in the parade and because it was so widely reported, more people began to support women's voting rights than ever before. Later in March, Alice Paul and other members of the NAWSA met with President Woodrow Wilson, but he said it was not time to get congressional approval for women to vote.

Missouri did not approve women's suffrage as its neighboring state, Kansas, had in 1912. Some people thought rights should be approved state-by-state. Others thought suffrage should be voted on at the federal level, meaning that the next step was for the United States Congress to approve women's suffrage.

The first picket line in front of the White House, Washington, DC, February 1917.

Alice Paul and Lucy Burns started a banner campaign in front of the White House to keep the issue in the minds of President Wilson and other politicians. They did not suspend their campaign during the Great War (what we now call World War I) even though many people thought that was disrespectful. The US did not enter the war until 1917, three years after the fighting had begun in Europe. Maye's childhood sweetheart, Fay Mills Corrough, enlisted. He was awarded the Purple Heart for service in the Argonne-Meuse battle.

In 1919, after Fay had returned from fighting overseas with a debilitating arm injury, he and Maye married. Others in the band married, too, and started families. That was the main reason that the Missouri Ladies Military Band dissolved.

Suffragists continued the fight before reaching their goal of women's suffrage for every state in the US. During those years, between 1913 and 1920, six states approved full voting rights for women: Montana, 1914; Nevada, 1914; New

York, 1917; Michigan, 1918; Oklahoma, 1918; and South Dakota, 1918. They joined the nine states already boasting full voting rights before the 1913 parade: Wyoming, 1890; Colorado, 1893; Utah, 1896; Idaho, 1896; Washington, 1910; California, 1911; Arizona, 1912; Kansas, 1912; and Oregon, 1912.

On August 18, 1920, Tennessee became the 36th state to ratify the 19th amendment, giving women in the United States the right to vote. The amendment reads:

"The right of citizens of the United States to vote shall not be denied or abridged by the United States or by any State on account of sex."

While this was a huge victory for women, it didn't include women of all races. One reason was that even though women of color fought hard for suffrage, they were not allowed to join white suffragist organizations. Another reason relates to having US citizenship, because only citizens can vote in US elections. So, several laws had to be passed for people of color to be able to vote. Until 1924, when the Indian Citizenship Act was passed, Native Peoples were not considered US citizens. Asian Americans were not allowed to vote until 1952, when the McCarran Walter Act was passed.

But Black Americans had to wait even longer. Forty-five years after the passage of the 19th amendment, the Voting Rights Act of 1965 was passed. It outlawed literacy tests—tests to see if people could read and write—that had been used to keep Black Americans from voting. The Voting

Rights Act did much more to protect voting so that all American citizens could vote without facing discrimination. This, along with the Civil Rights Act of 1964, helped to prevent unfair treatment against Black people. In the US South, this discrimination was actually legal! These laws were known as "Jim Crow" laws. Even today, we are still fighting so that every vote will be counted.

Maye played a small part, along with thousands of other women and men, in gaining voting rights. She had the courage to stand up for her beliefs, and it had a ripple effect. She didn't know how or if one small act would affect the future. When she began, she didn't know if marching with the Ladies Band would help women's suffrage succeed. In 1920, when Maye heard the news, she was shopping about 10 miles south of Maryville in the Arkoe General Store. And she got up on the counter and danced!

The Missouri Ladies Military Band

Twenty-three members of the Missouri Ladies Military Band traveled to Washington, DC. Of the nine bands in the parade, the Missouri Ladies Military Band was the only one comprised solely of women.

B-flat clarinet:	Mary O'Brien, Anna Dougan, Ora Quinn, Helen Young
E-flat clarinet:	Margaret Conway
Piccolo:	Helen Rowley
Alto saxophone:	Lela Caudle, Mrs. Del Thompson
B-flat tenor saxophone:	Myrtle Lanning
B-flat baritone saxophone:	Hazel Vandervoot
Cornet:	Grace O'Brien, Mary Evans, Hazel Garrett, Velma Lanning, Gertrude Kirch

Slide trombone: Maye Shipps
E-flat bass horn: Florence Shipps
B-flat bass horn: Mrs. Velma Gray Johnson
Snare drums: Esther Eversole
Bass drum: Orlena Helpley
Cymbals: Elizabeth Nash
Former member, Selma Young, Creston, Iowa, joined the band for the trip
Band Director: Alma Nash

Vera Maye Shipps, band member, slide trombone, married her childhood sweetheart, Fay Mills Corrough, in 1919. A homemaker, she had a son and a daughter. She voted in every election she could after the 19th amendment was ratified. Maye's son and grandson played her precious trombone. She wouldn't trust its care to anyone else. Maye lived to be 96 and attended several anniversary celebrations of the march on Washington.

Florence Shipps, band member, tuba, married J. Frank Gray in 1914. A graduate of Northwest Normal School (now Northwest Missouri State University), she was a teacher and mother of a son. She lived to be 98.

Orlena Helpley, band member, bass drum, married Rodolph Richmond Staples in 1917. Orlena cast her first vote in 1922 and in every election until 1977, when mobility issues prevented her from leaving home. She was instrumental in creating the Atchison County Health

Department and was involved in Daughters of the American Revolution. She lived until 1983, age 90.

Alma Nash, band director, grew up in Maryville, where her father was a doctor and her mother, a nurse. She owned The School of Banjo, Mandolin, and Guitar. Alma moved to Kansas City, Missouri, in 1918, where she played drums in the orchestra at the Doric Theater. Throughout her lifetime, Alma taught 4,000 students to play musical instruments. In later years, she said the march on Washington was the most memorable event of her life. She died in 1965 at age 83.

If you have information about the other women in the band, please contact the Nodaway County Historical Museum:
110 North Walnut, Box 324, Maryville, MO 64468
Telephone: (660) 582-8176
Website: https://nodawaymuseum.wixsite.com/nchs
Email: nodawaymuseumresearch@embarqmail.com

Index

Anthony, Susan B.   39, 41
Burns, Lucy   41, 43
Corrough, Fay Mills   43, 47
Daily Democrat-Forum   16
Fort Myer Cavalry   34
Gellhorn, Edna F.   15, 23
Helpley, Orlena   12, 47
Jones, "General" Rosalie   42
Kansas City Times   9
Mary Villemo   21
Maryville, Missouri   8, 9, 11, 15, 16, 18, 20, 21, 28, 37, 39, 40, 45, 48
Milholland, Inez   29, 30
Moberly, Missouri   23
Nash, Alma   9, 10, 13, 14, 15, 17, 18, 20, 23, 25, 32, 33, 37, 47, 48
Nash, Elizabeth   18, 22, 47
National American Woman Suffrage Association (NAWSA)   9, 30, 31, 36, 41
National Women's Rights Convention   41
Paul, Alice   41, 42, 43
Pittsburg, Pennsylvania   26
Quinn, Ora   11, 19, 23, 24, 27, 30, 46
Shaw, Dr. Anna Howard   36
Shipps, Florence   9, 18, 26, 47
Sousa, John Philip   12

St. Louis Star   24
St. Louis, Missouri   15, 20, 23, 24, 37
Stanton, Elizabeth Cady   40, 41
Steubenville, Ohio   25
Sylvester, Major Richard   42
Wabash Railroad Depot   11, 18
Washington, DC   8, 14, 19, 24, 27, 28, 32, 39, 41, 42, 43, 46, 47, 48
Wilson, Woodrow   8, 28, 36, 41 42, 43
World War I   43

Image Credits

Front Cover: Missouri Ladies Military Band, Bain News Service, Publisher. Woman band - Suffrage parade., 1913. March 3 date created or published later by Bain. Photograph. https://www.loc.gov/item/2014691491/.

Back Cover: Missouri Ladies Military Band in Washington, DC before the parade, Courtesy National Woman's Party at the Belmont-Paul Women's Equality National Monument.

1. Vera Maye Shipps closeup, Courtesy Nodaway County Historical Museum.
2. Maryville, Missouri, early 1900s, Courtesy Nodaway County Historical Museum.
3. Alma Nash postcard, Courtesy Nodaway County Historical Museum.
4. Trombone, photo by Mary Seat, Grant City, Missouri.
5. Wabash Railroad Depot, Maryville, Missouri, Courtesy Colby Lamb, Maryville, Missouri.
6. Missouri Ladies Military Band, seated outside, Courtesy Nodaway County Historical Museum.
7. Bell, Alexander Graham, and Mabel Hubbard Bell. Telegram from Alexander Graham Bell to Mabel Hubbard Bell. 1913. Manuscript/Mixed Material. https://www.loc.gov/item/magbell.04310203/.
8. Missouri Ladies Military Band, seated in a concert hall, Courtesy Nodaway County Historical Museum.

9. Mrs. George Gellhorn, [League of Women Voters of St. Louis Addenda, 1916-1977 (S0530), The State Historical Society of Missouri, Manuscript Collection-St. Louis].
10. Daily Democrat Forum, March 3, 1913. Courtesy Phil Cobb, owner, Maryville Forum, Maryville, Missouri.
11. Missouri Ladies Military Band, seated at the Wabash Railway Station, Courtesy Nodaway County Historical Museum.
12. Map of the train route from Maryville to St. Louis. Courtesy, The State Historical Society of Missouri. https://digital.shsmo.org/digital/collection/Maps/id/32.
13. Postcard of the Ladies Band and song "Mary Villemo," Courtesy Colby Lamb, Maryville, Missouri.
14. Railroad ticket and punch, photo by Amy Houts, Nodaway County Historical Museum.
15. United States map with Railway line from St. Louis to Washington DC. Library of Congress. Patterson, S. C, and Pennsylvania Railroad. Map of the Pennsylvania Railroad and its connections. [Philadelphia, 1889] Map. https://www.loc.gov/item/98688765/.
16. La Belle Ironworks, Courtesy the Ohio County Public Library Archives, Wheeling, WV.
17. Detroit Publishing Co., Publisher. Dining car, D.L. & W. R.R. Delaware, Lackawanna and Western Railroad., None. [Between 1900 and 1905] Photograph. https://www.loc.gov/item/2016811429/.

18. Bain News Service, Publisher. Suffrage parade, Inez Milholland. District of Columbia United States Washington D.C. Washington D.C, 1913. [March date created or published later by Bain] Photograph. https://www.loc.gov/item/2014691461/.
19. Head of suffrage parade in Washington, D.C., Mar. 3. Washington D.C, 1913. March 3. Photograph. https://www.loc.gov/item/97500042/.
20. Missouri Ladies Military Band, Bain News Service, Publisher. Woman band - Suffrage parade., 1913. March 3 date created or published later by Bain. Photograph. https://www.loc.gov/item/2014691491/.
21. Suffragette parade, Washington, D.C., on March 3., ca. 1913. Photograph. https://www.loc.gov/item/2005693330/.
22. L & M Ottenheimer, Baltimore, Md. Liberty and her Attendants - Suffragette's Tableau in Front of Treasury Bldg. March 3,- Washington, D.C. United States Washington D.C, 1913. Mar. 3. Photograph. https://www.loc.gov/item/mnwp000279/.
23. Keppler, Udo J., Artist. Woodrow Wilson / Keppler, 1912. N.Y.: Published by Keppler & Schwarzmann, Puck Building. Photograph. https://www.loc.gov/item/2011649367/.
24. Susan B. Anthony sitting and reading a book., ca. 1900. Photograph. https://www.loc.gov/item/2004671946/.

25. Dale, Benjamin M., -1951, Artist, and U.S. Records League Of Women Voters. Official program - Woman suffrage procession, Washington, D.C. March 3,/ Dale. United States Washington D.C, 1913. Photograph. https://www.loc.gov/item/94507639/.
26. Alice Paul., ca. 1918. Photograph. https://www.loc.gov/item/2004670382/.
27. Lucy Burns, half portrait, seated., ca. 1913. Photograph. https://www.loc.gov/item/2016650622/
28. *The first picket line - College day in the picket line.* Washington D.C, 1917. Feb. Photograph. https://www.loc.gov/item/97500299/.
29. Missouri Ladies Military Band, Corn Contest Days Concert, Courtesy of Nodaway County Historical Museum.

Bibliography

Blakemore, Erin. "1920: The Suffragists." *Time Magazine*, March 16/23, 2020.

Brown, Tony. "Museum to Mark Women's Band Centennial." *Maryville (MO) Daily Forum*, February 14, 2013, Section A, 1-2.

Cooper, Martha L. *Suffrage Comes to the Women of Nodaway County, Missouri*. Maryville, MO: Accent Printing, 1997.

Eckert, Opal. "Maryville Band Hailed As 1st," *Maryville (MO) Daily Forum*, August, 18, 1984.

Gambino, Megan, "Document Deep Dive: A Historic Moment in the Fight for Women's Voting Rights" *Smithsonian Magazine*, March 1, 2013. http://www.smithsonianmag.com/history-archaeology/Document-Deep-Dive-A-Historic-Moment-in-the-Fight-for-Womens-Voting-Rights-194203341.html.

Kuehl, Claudia. "Woman Played to Beat the Ban on Vote," *The Kansas City (MO) Star*, August 26, 1984.

LeHigh Valley, Pennsylvania Railroad Car Dining Service Menu 1913. https://lovemenuart.com/products/lehigh-valley-railroad-dining-car-service-1913.

Library of Congress. "America the Beautiful." https://www.loc.gov/item/ihas.200000001/. Accessed August 8, 2017.

Library of Congress. "Marching for the Vote: Remembering the Woman Suffrage Parade of 1913." http://memory.loc.gov/ammem/awhhtml/aw01e/aw01e.html. Accessed March 11, 2013.

Library of Congress. "The Official Program Women Suffrage Procession." http://memory.loc.gov/cgi-bin/ampage?collId=rbpe&fileName=rbpe20/rbpe208/20801600/rbpe20801600.db&recNum=0&itemLink=r?ammem/rbpebib:@field(NUMBER+@band(rbpe+20801600))&linkText=0. Accessed September 20, 2016.

Mann, Laurie. "Timeline of Women's Suffrage in the United States." Women's Sites Resources. Last modified March 8, 2017. http://dpsinfo.com/women/history/timeline.html.

Maryville, Missouri Catalogue Book. School of Banjo, Mandolin, and Guitar, The. 114 ½ South Buchanan. Alma Nash, Directress. Nodaway County Historical Museum, Maryville, Missouri.

Maryville, Missouri City Address Book, 1906. Nodaway County Historical Museum, Maryville, Missouri.

Maryville (MO) Daily Forum. "Fay Mills Corrough, Obituary." May 14, 1971, 8. https://www.newspapers.com/newspage/83925714/.

Maryville (MO) Daily Forum. "Florence Irene Gray, Obituary." February 23, 1987.

Maryville (MO) Daily Forum. "Vera Maye Shipps Corrough, Obituary." November 13, 1989.

Missouri Women: Women of the Past, Inspiring Women Today. "Alma Nash & Her Band." Last modified November 16, 2010. http://missouriwomen.org/2010/11/16/alma-nash-her-maryville-ladies-marching-band/.

National Parks Service, "Between Two Worlds: Black Women and the Fight for Voting Rights." https://www.nps.gov/articles/black-women-and-the-fight-for-voting-rights.htm. Accessed July 8, 2020.

National Constitution Center. "Centuries of Citizenship: A Constitutional Timeline," http://constitutioncenter.org/timeline/html/cw08_12159.html. Accessed September 28, 2016.

Newton, Ken. "Act of Courage Helped Stir History." *St. Joseph (MO) News-Press*, March 7, 2013, Section 1, 1, 8.

Nicholson, Larry. "Her Ladies Band Helped Suffragette Cause." *The Kansas City (MO) Star*, January 8, 1966.

O'Neil, Tim. "Missouri Suffragists Make Final Push for Right to Vote." *St. Louis (MO) Post-Dispatch*, September 13, 2014. http://www.stltoday.com/news/local/govt-and-politics/look-back-missouri-suffragists-make-final-push-for-right-to/article_f1abd693-5eb0-5869-9f91-6c488d30454a.html.

O Say Can You See? Stories from the National Museum of American History; "Guest Post: Three Objects from the 1913 Woman Suffrage Parade." Blog entry by Elspeth Kursh, March 1, 2013. http://americanhistory.si.edu/blog/2013/03/guest-post-three-objects-from-the-1913-woman-suffrage-parade.html.

Panetta, Grace, and Olivia Reaney. "Today is National Voter Registration Day. The evolution of American voting rights in 242 years shows how far we've come — and how far we still have to go." *Business Insider*, September 24, 2019. https://www.businessinsider.com/when-women-got-the-right-to-vote-american-voting-rights-timeline-2018-10 Accessed July 8,2020.

Shipps, Vera Maye. "Excerpts from Her Diary, 1910-1913." Nodaway County Historical Museum, Maryville, Missouri.

"Staples, Orlena A. *Helpley*." Find a Grave. https://www.findagrave.com/cgi-bin/.

"Staples, Rodolph Richmond." Find a Grave. http://www.findagrave.com/cgi-bin/fg.cgi?page=gr&GRid=19526052. Accessed April 29, 2013.

Sullivan, Dr. Jill M., "Town Bands." Arizona State University. http://www.public.asu.edu/~jmsulli/Webpages/townbands.htm. Accessed April 29, 2013.

Sullivan, Dr. Jill M., "Women's Military Band Research." Arizona State University. http://www.public.asu.edu/~jmsulli/Webpages/military.html. Accessed April 29, 2013.

Taylor, Alan. "The 1913 Women's Suffrage Parade." *The Atlantic*, March 1, 2013. http://www.theatlantic.com/infocus/2013/03/100-years-ago-the-1913-womens-suffrage-parade/100465/.

The Washington (DC) Times. "Roster and Route of the Suffrage Pageant." March 3, 1913, evening edition, Section 1, 1.

US Department of Agriculture Weather Bureau, Monthly Weather Review, Washington, DC, 1914.

Women's History Museum. "Press Coverage - 1913 Suffrage Parade in Washington, DC." https://www.youtube.com/watch?v=bi3mxt1Xhyk. Accessed September 28, 2016.

World Heritage Encyclopedia. "Woman Suffrage Parade of 1913." http://self.gutenberg.org/articles/eng/Woman_Suffrage_Parade_of_1913. Accessed September 29, 2016.

Wood, Jacki, "Marching for a Cause: Program to Celebrate Maryville Ladies Band." *Nodaway [County, MO] News Leader*, February 28, 2013, Section 1, 1-2.

In addition, the author conducted two interviews:

Melissa Middleswart (Retired 30-year librarian, Rolling Hills Library, Savannah, MO, local historian and Alma Nash expert), May 16, 2013.

Thomas Carneal (Professor Emeritus of History, Northwest Missouri State University, Maryville, MO, Nodaway County Historian), May 16, 2013.